Pebble™ Plus

Animal Homes

Rabbits and Their Burrows

by Linda Tagliaferro

Consulting Editor: Gail Saunders-Smith, Ph.D.

Consultant: Henry Bulluck, Animal Keeper
Western North Carolina Nature Center
Asheville, North Carolina

Capstone
press

Mankato, Minnesota

Pebble Plus is published by Capstone Press
151 Good Counsel Drive, P.O. Box 669, Mankato, Minnesota 56002
www.capstonepress.com

1 2 3 4 5 6 09 08 07 06 05 04

Library of Congress Cataloging-in-Publication Data
Tagliaferro, Linda.
    Rabbits and their burrows / by Linda Tagliaferro.
    p. cm.—(Pebble Plus, animal homes)
    Summary: Simple text and photographs describe rabbits and the burrows in which they live.
    Includes bibliographical references (p. 23) and index.
    ISBN 0-7368-2384-0 (hardcover)
    1. Rabbits—Habitations—Juvenile literature. 2. Animal burrowing—Juvenile literature.
[1. Rabbits—Habitations. 2. Rabbits—Habits and behavior.] I. Title. II. Series.
QL737.L32T34 2004
599.32—dc22   2003013427

Editorial Credits
Martha E. H. Rustad, editor; Linda Clavel, series designer; Deirdre Barton and Wanda Winch,
    photo researchers; Karen Risch, product planning editor

Photo Credits
Bruce Coleman Inc./Gary Meszaros, 20–21; Gary Zahm, 4–5; Pat & Rae Hagan, 19
Corbis/Tony Hamblin/Frank Lane Picture Agency, cover
Corel, 10–11
Minden Pictures/Jim Brandenburg, 8–9
Tom and Pat Leeson, 7
Unicorn Stock Photos/Jack Milchanowski, 13; Ted Rose, 14–15
Visuals Unlimited/Gary Meszaros, 1; Raymond Coleman, 17

Note to Parents and Teachers

The Animal Homes series supports national science standards related to life science. This book describes and illustrates rabbits and their burrows. The images support early readers in understanding the text. The repetition of words and phrases helps early readers learn new words. This book also introduces early readers to subject-specific vocabulary words, which are defined in the Glossary. Early readers may need assistance to read some words and to use the Table of Contents, Glossary, Read More, Internet Sites, and Index/Word List sections of the book.

Word Count: 136
Early-Intervention Level: 15

Table of Contents

Making Homes

Rabbits make homes
called burrows or nests.

Some rabbits dig underground
holes called burrows. Many
burrows together make
a warren. Rabbits dig with
their front paws.

Some rabbits dig holes

on top of the ground.

These holes are called nests.

Rabbits dig for one or two hours. They line their burrows or nests with grass and with fur from their bodies.

Bunnies

Young rabbits are called bunnies or kits. A female rabbit gives birth to about five bunnies in a burrow or nest.

Bunnies stay warm in
the burrow or nest. Bunnies
are born without fur.

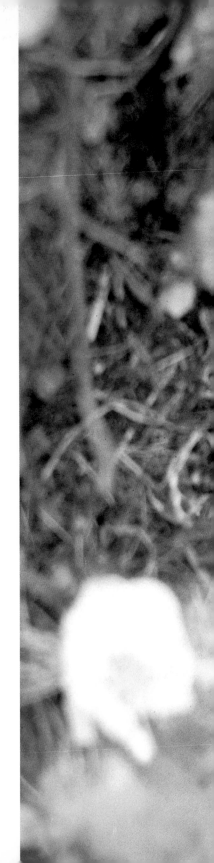

15

Newborn bunnies cannot see
or hear. They stay safe in
the burrow or nest.

Hiding

Rabbits hide in their burrows or nests. Hungry animals cannot find the rabbits and their bunnies.

A Good Home

Burrows and nests are safe homes for rabbits and their bunnies.

Glossary

bunny—a young rabbit; female rabbits have about four litters of about five bunnies each year; bunnies are also called kits.

burrow—a tunnel or hole in the ground dug by an animal; some rabbits raise their young in burrows.

fur—the soft, thick coat of an animal; rabbit fur can be black, gray, brown, or white.

nest—a hole or dent in the ground where rabbits raise their young

paw—the foot of an animal

warren—a group of burrows

Read More

Jacobs, Lee. *Rabbits.* Wild America. San Diego: Blackbirch Press, 2002.

Swanson, Diane. *Rabbits and Hares.* Welcome to the World of Animals. Milwaukee: Gareth Stevens, 2002.

Whitehouse, Patricia. *Rabbits.* Under My Feet. Chicago: Heinemann Library, 2003.

Internet Sites

FactHound offers a safe, fun way to find Internet sites related to this book. All of the sites on FactHound have been researched by our staff.

Here's how:

1. Visit *www.facthound.com*

2. Type in this special code **0736823840** for age-appropriate sites. Or enter a search word related to this book for a more general search.

3. Click on the **Fetch It** button.

FactHound will fetch the best sites for you!

Index/Word List